Dragonflies Are Super Bugs

Story by Clare Mishica
Illustrations by Ryan Durney

Dragonflies are super bugs!
Dragonflies see better than any
other bug. They can see you
from 20 feet away.

Dragonflies can fly fast too.
They fly up to 60 miles an hour.
That's how fast you go in a car.

Dragonflies can do flying tricks too. They can fly backwards or sideways.

They can even stop in the air,
just like a helicopter.

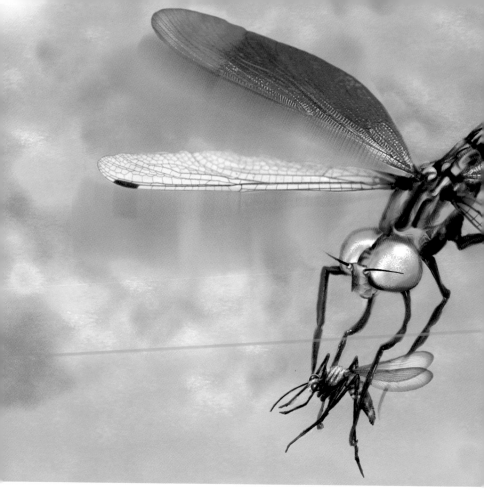

Dragonflies can even eat
while they are flying.

They eat lots of flies and
mosquitoes. A dragonfly can
eat 600 bugs in a day.

But a dragonfly will not bite you.
This super bug is a super friend.